How to Apocalypse

Hassan Rasheed

ISBN

978-1-008-94564-7

Printed in the United States of America
By Lulu.com

Prolog

Carl G. Jung the famed psychiatrist (26 July 1875 – 6 June 1961) said, "As far as we can decern, the sole purpose of human existence is to kindle a light in the darkness of mere being."

In contrast and as far as I can decern, the sole purpose of human existence is to discover the light of mere being. Humans don't know that yet but it will become apparent one day. My job here is to hurry that process along. (2021)

Chapter 1

The Humans

Conventional wisdom has it, humans are more intelligent than any other species on Earth. The evidence includes that our brains are proportionately heavier to body weight than those of other species especially the frontal lobes. Human also have the ability to communicate in several ways, design and make tools, accumulate wealth and have a so-called higher standard of living than all other species. Most of all is our possession of a conscience and self-awareness which we think other species definitely don't have.

"So, God created man in his own image, in the image of God created he him; male and female created he them. And God blessed them, and God said unto them, Be fruitful, and multiply, and replenish the earth, and subdue it: and have dominion over the fish of the sea, and over the fowl of the air, and over every living thing that moveth upon the earth. And God said, Behold, I have given you every herb bearing seed, which is upon the face of all the earth, and every tree, in the which is the fruit of a tree

yielding seed; to you it shall be for meat. And to every beast of the earth, and to every fowl of the air, and to every thing that creepeth upon the earth, wherein there is life, I have given every green herb for meat: and it was so."

Clearly, the Jewish-Christian God has declared humans as more important than all other creatures on Earth and that all resources are at the human's disposal. This feeds the ego of humanity that then makes them feel they are more intelligent than any other species on Earth. In addition, humanity perceives itself at the top of what we now call the food chain where humans eat the meat of the beast that in turn eats the herb of the field. Furthermore, God has given humans the power over all other resources.

Major contemporary religions reflect the importance of humans to themselves. In other words, it is the human ego's way of self-preservation by declaring itself more important than any other species or mineral.

In summary, humans have three qualities; one is their belief that they have superior intelligence; the second is the belief they are superior beings; the third is they have power over all others and things.

Chapter 2

The Chain

However, there is some work being done on the relationships between plant species in a forest. For example, plants of different species share resources and it is becoming abundantly clear life on Earth is like a complex circular chain. Each link is as important as the next. If one link dies, the chain is degraded and we are all in danger of death since the chain is broken. The conclusion is that all species including humans are equally important to our planet Earth.

The flawed perception that modern humans are more important than any other form of life on Earth has led humans to think of themselves at the highest link of the food chain. Modern humans also have the perception that the chain is simple, that it proceeds from the top link to the bottom one with perhaps a few side branches. This flawed perception hinders them from seeing the whole complex picture.

In reality the chain on first order is circular. Meaning that there is no start or end, no top or bottom link nor is there an intelligent link or a dumb one. The chain is also very complex. It has many circular side chains. The chain is more or less like a solid sphere where no one circular chain can be distinguished from another.

Nature is complex. Modern humans are incapable of grasping its complexity. The reality is that they are part of it and of equal value to all other parts. Modern humans must rid themselves of the notion they are more intelligent or better than any other life form. Modern humans must become humble and respectful of the original order and boundaries of nature.

Chapter 3

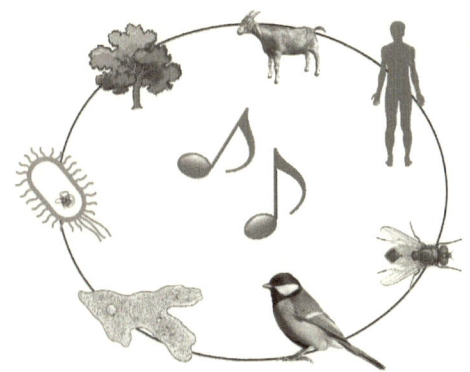

The Cyclical Nature of Life

Plants capture the energy from the rays of the Sun and use it to uptake minerals from the soil. Both mineral and energy then cascade through all species on Earth until the energy is used up to do mechanical or chemical work and the minerals returned to the Earth once again for plants to pick up using the next batch of solar rays. This is the way it started and the way it has continued on this planet for billions of years. The result is the glorious biota that we all can see today.

Life on planet Earth is meant to be a cascade of the Sun's energy through the different species where the top soil minerals are recycled and entropy is held at bay. But when modern humans appeared on the scene chaos broke loose. They discovered alternate energy sources and were not beholding to the Sun anymore. They dug deeper into the Earth scattering its minerals speeding up the advancement of entropy as if aliens landed on Earth in the past and implanted a foreign seed in the brain of a tribe of humans that eventually took over.

Modern humans appear as bullies swaggering their way throughout planet Earth without regard to its original inhabitants in pursuit of dominance which they call their happiness. They don't understand their pursuit of their kind of happiness is at the expense and demise of all other species.

True Earthly recycling involves many species in tandem and/or in parallel each using whatever energy and minerals they can extract from the recycled material for their livelihood then passing what they can't use on to the next species in cyclic chain. The flora uptakes minerals from the soil and capture the energy from the rays of the Sun which then cascade down to animals, insects and microbes were the original minerals in the life-giving resource are then given up once again to the soil for plants to pick up again.

In contrast, when modern humans recycle paper into more paper, they don't return any minerals to the earth. In addition, the chemicals humans use to convert used paper to usable paper pollute the rivers, streams and in general the environments with chemicals such as dioxins to name just one family of many.

Chapter 4

Life and Death

The majority of plant, animal, insect and microbe population numbers on Earth were relatively stable in the past. This means their relative reproductive rates are equal to the relative death rates. Reproductive rates are dependent on the ability to gather life sustaining and reproductive resources such as food and shelter. Death rates are dependent on predation, disease and old age.

Without these life and death balances there will be a runaway population count either increasing or decreasing. The modern human population is an example. With technology increasing the ability to gather life's sustaining and birthing resources coupled with the escape from predation, disease and encroaching old age (through the medical sciences) the population is in a run-away increase in numbers because birth rate is greater than the death rate.

There once was no birth without death and no death without rebirth. Nature takes care of the ones we lose by amending them to new life.

Nature has learned to eliminate one individual for the benefit of the group if the population grows to 11 individuals in an environment that can only support 10 at a subsistence level. This is done by disease, parasite, famine or predation.

Death by old age is a necessity. It is so for two reasons. The first is to replace an old body that has lived a full life and the cost of maintaining it further is greater than its benefit to the group. The second is that if the environment is changing in a fundamental way and so the population must also change in a similar way perhaps requiring changes to the genetic code through mutations. The previous ways of dealing with the environment must give way to new ways through new births reflecting these changes genetically.

Death due to an abnormality in an individual is preferred by nature to avoid the abnormality from becoming a burden to the rest of the group or population.

And death is not something to fear or feel sorry about. It is natural to die for you make way for new births when you do. Your body is not wasted away but becomes the source of a new beginning. It is as if you are resurrected in the same or a million other forms. The same goes for a people, a species, an ecosystem, a planetary biota, a planet, and a start system like ours when consumed by a black hole. All will not perish but be transformed.

Chapter 5

Dead Ends

There is one thing we must realize here and that is nature makes no promises. There are many examples of what is known as evolutionary dead ends in which a species simply ends up dead when its habitat no longer exists or is unable to support it.

An example is The Equus Gigantism, or giant horse, that was for many years considered only to be an artificial cave painting of a hippopotamus, until when the bones of several were exposed. This horse differed from the modern horse. Its forepaws being somewhat briefer than its hindquarters. This gave it the look of having been exaggeratedly lowered in the front. It had very large feet in the back with huge muscles, seemingly giving it greater power and quickening ability for escaping its enemies.

Early cave images usually depict a human male riding one of these giant horses as numerous large-breasted human females gaze on him in admiration. It also appears that this giant horse was often times decorated with flaming torches in the back, large funnels directing air to the nostrils so that the animal can breathe better, and showy gold pinwheels decorating its knees. Many times, a huge bass drum was also fastened to the horse producing earth-shaking thuds.

Examination of the skeletal structure of this giant horse shows that this creature could easily accelerate to high speeds even with the extra loads. It is thought that Equus Gigantism went extinct because it drank too much, ate too much, and left too much defecate material polluting the settlements of early man.

Chapter 6

The Apocalypse

Current evidence indicates we are on the cusp of a catastrophic global biotic dead end possibly returning climate conditions back to what existed 600 million years ago where global temperatures were higher as well as having a different atmospheric chemistry. There is no question human activity is driving this dead end by exhuming ancient remains and resurrecting the conditions in existence back then. It is as if nature is saying the current conditions are not sustainable and Earth needs to reset and return to a previous maintainable environment.

To explain how and why all this is happening we will talk about the nature of a population bloom in the context of an algae bloom then turn our attention to the human population bloom.

The Algae Bloom
The term bloom refers to the explosion of algae density in a pond. In order to understand what an algae bloom does, we first must understand how a pond of water operates. A

pond naturally occurring in the forest consists of a pond bottom made out of soil or clay that is a depression in the ground filled with water. On top of the water is air. When algae grow in water, it receives sunlight from above and nutrients from the water and the soil beneath. As the algae grow, mature and die, they sink to the bottom of the pond. There, bacteria decompose the algae matter and release key elements that then circulate in the pond water nourishing subsequent generations of algae.

Algae blooms in ponds are common. They occur when the conditions are right for algae to take a sudden or prolonged burst of growth. This burst is usually due to an increase in one or more chemical resources in the water essential for algae growth such as compounds containing phosphate.

Most blooms are benign to the water system. The water might turn a bright green color for a few days or a week or so. The algae that bloomed die and sink to the bottom of the pond when the chemical or chemicals that initiated the bloom are consumed.

Some water systems experience long blooms. These may last from a month to two or longer so long as the chemical resources responsible for the bloom continue to come into the water system, such as affluent from sewer systems. This can be devastating to the water system's biota and cycles because the increase in the number of algae corpses being consumed by bacteria, which is an Oxygen consumer, will cause the lake to become oxygen deficient for many plants and animal species, which in turn die off. This type of bloom chokes life out of the lake that will eventually die, culminating in aerobic bacteria jumping into action, producing foul smells like rotten eggs associated with stagnant water systems, after most if not all oxygen is consumed.

You would think that even if the chemical sources that promoted the bloom in the first place continue to flow into the pond the bloom will continue indefinitely, but on the contrary, the bloom will eventually die off and sink to the bottom of the water system if other chemical resources necessary for life are depleted as a result of the bloom. You see, algae depend on many chemical resources present in the water system and when one or more of these are depleted, the bloom can't continue and dies off sinking to the bottom where the bacteria go to work.

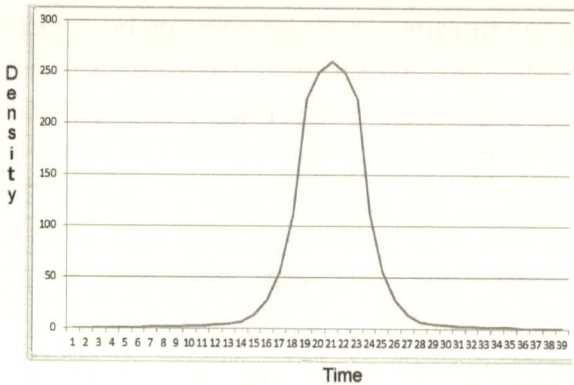

The density of algae in a pond undergoing a long bloom.

To bring back a pond that has experienced a bloom, we need to take out the algae, plant matter, and animals that died during the boom and their associated decomposition bacteria. In addition, all sources of chemicals responsible for the bloom must be stopped from entering the pond. Only then will enough oxygen be reabsorbed by the pond from the air above, allowing fish, plants and algae to grow once again and continue the lifecycle of the pond.

Mankind is believed to be undergoing a "bloom" which carries with it a mass extinction of over 50% of all life on Earth. Current civilizations are highly dependent on fossil fuels that drive the consumption of other resources which are not limitless or are on a delicate balance on this finite Earth. The signs are all around us, which include the destruction of the habitats of countless species that we depend on for our own habitat sustenance.

Underlying this argument is the idea that we as humans and our habitat are no different than the algae in the pond. It is all a matter of chemical reactions that follow physical laws of which we have no control. Whether it is phosphates or fossil fuels that caused or cause the long "bloom," the end results are similar.

In these modern times, we face a whole new set of challenges that differ from the challenges faced by our Greek ancestors such as Socrates and Plato. In those early times, the challenges were those of aggregating people together into cities that are under the control of fair and acceptable laws. Today we face a whole new set of problems related to the biological "success" of our species.

The Human Population Bloom

With these four major technologies (cooperation, money, utilization of fossil energy and medicine) working at full steam, the human population of the Earth has exploded from a few tribes in Africa 300,000 years ago to a global population level of around 7 billion people today (see chart below).

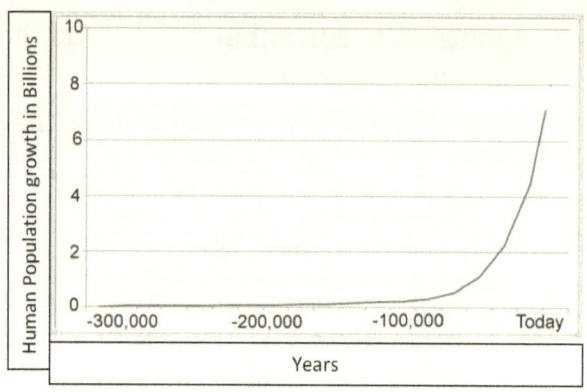

The population growth of humans through time.

We might ask at this point, "Are there any side effects to the apparent success of humankind?"

The following are a few examples of the negative effects of humankind upon the planet Earth:

Extinctions

We are in a biodiversity crisis. The fastest mass extinction in Earth's history is happening right now, largely due to human activities.

There is no doubt in the minds of biologists that the Earth is losing a race with time to save its precious cargo. In 1993, Harvard Biologist

E.O. Wilson estimated that Earth is losing about 30,000 species per year or 3 species per hour. This means that 700,000 species have gone extinct since this estimate was made. This biodiversity crisis is snowballing and many experts predict a sixth mass extinction is on the horizon.

There is no doubt that humans are the direct cause of this habitat stress and species destruction in the modern world through such activities as transformation of the landscape (through agriculture, construction and uncontrolled forestry practices), overexploitation of species (by overhunting game species), pollution, human over-population, and the introduction of alien species into existing habitats.

The Habitats

With the domestication of plants and animal, more and more lands are required to support this human activity, which is also a loss of habitat for animal and plant species of no interest to humans.

For example, in the southern United States of America, beef cattle are raised on ranges making them compete with other indigenous species that naturally occur there. This competition is aided by humankind's ability to shoot with a gun or poison those species that are undesirable to them.

As with pollinating insects, we will find out later that all animals, insects and plants are critical to the health of the planet Earth.

Soil Erosion and Degradation (Eckholm, P Erik)

Natural processes moved rocks from their resting places down hills and gullies using wind and water currents causing them to collide with other rocks. All this movement resulted in the formation of soils about 450 million years ago when plants started to take root after evolving from simpler organisms. Since then, soils have moved by the actions of water or wind, known as erosion.

In general, this erosion removes soil from an area at roughly the same rate as soil formation. A far more recent problem is the loss of soil at a much faster rate than its formation. That is the result of humankind's actions such as overgrazing or unsuitable cultivation practices.

These actions leave the land vulnerable and unprotected. For example, during times of erosive rainfall or windstorms, soil may be detached and transported away and deposited in undesirable locations.

Soil may also be degraded, which includes salinization, nutrient loss and compaction, all due to human activities that include agriculture and construction.

The result of soil erosion and degradation is the reduction in soil fertility and its support of living plants and animals, including humans.

Deforestation (Tucker, Richard P. and J. F. Richards)

It has been estimated that about half of the Earth's mature tropical forests—between 2.9 million to 3 million square miles of the original 5.8 million to 6.2 million square miles that until 1947 covered the planet, have now been destroyed. Some scientists have predicted that unless significant measures such as seeking out and protecting current old growth forests are taken on a worldwide basis, by 2030 there will only be 10% remaining, with another 10% in a degraded condition; 80% will have been lost and with them hundreds of thousands of irreplaceable species.

In addition, with the loss of forests, so is their loss of habitat for millions if not billions of plant, animal and insect species.

Insecticides (Alexandra Ludka of ABC News, Mar 15, 2012 6:15pm)

Through most of history insects have been loathed. From locusts to termites and the Bol weevil they have gained a reputation of being detrimental to the interests of humankind. It wasn't until recent history that some insects were discovered to be useful and helpful to humankind.

The bee is just one example. It wasn't until its beneficial effects on pollination were discovered that an appreciation of its services to humankind were recognized. Today, bees are in danger from insecticides used to protect plants from other insects and fungi.

Honeybees are critical for pollinating food crops. Scientists say the disruption of pollination could dramatically affect entire ecosystems. There are many more insects and insect larvae that are critical to human existence.

The Depletion of Global Fisheries (Clark, Colin W.)

A report entitled "Status and Solutions for the World's Unassessed Fisheries" by the Sustainable Fisheries Group (SFG) has confirmed the suspicions held by many researchers that nearly 80 percent of the world's fisheries are in steep decline. The reasons for this decline are overfishing caused by many factors that include uninformed political pressure that tends to dominate the decision-making process and the problem of the unmanaged commons where there is policy for management. Over time, this can lead fisheries to collapse.

Invasive Species

Invasive species are species that are transferred from one ecosystem to another, competing with native ones and taking over their habitats. An increase in global trade has increased the number of plant and animal species that are carried from one part of the globe to another legally, illegally or accidentally. Some of these species become invasive and cause havoc to the destination ecosystems, often reducing biodiversity and ecological balance.

Hazardous and Toxic Waste (Brown, Michael Harold)

Hazardous waste poses substantial or potential threats to public health and the environment. Worldwide, the United Nations Environmental Program (UNEP) estimated the production of more than 400 million tons of hazardous waste universally each year by industrialized countries, with about 4 million tons shipped across international boundaries. The majority of the transfers occurring between industrialized countries to developing nations for disposal are because of the rising cost of disposing of hazardous waste in the home country. Disposal consists of storage either above or below ground, leaving a legacy for future generations. In the case of biological toxins, they are incinerated and, if they are not, are stored or released into the air.

Water Depletion (Anisfeld, Shimon C.)

Groundwater is a valuable resource throughout the world. Where surface water, such as lakes and rivers, are scarce or inaccessible, groundwater supplies many of the hydrologic needs of people everywhere. Sustained groundwater pumping as the result of overpopulation causes groundwater depletion and is a key issue associated with groundwater use. Many areas of the world are experiencing groundwater depletion.

Pumping groundwater faster than its recharge rate can have some negative effects on the environment and the people who make use of the water: Lowering of the water table causes the cost of drilling and pumping water to be more expensive.

The cause of the reduction of water in streams and lakes is partly due to groundwater depletion and reduction of the water table.

Land subsidence occurs when water is removed from the soil. As a result, the soil collapses and compacts.

The cause of deterioration of water quality in fresh groundwater supplies is saltwater intrusion from oceans, seas, very deep groundwater sources and water below oceans that are saline. (USGS Fact Sheet) (USGS Circular 1186)

Further, rainwater overuse is a major issue in recent times due to the drought in California as a result of the decrease rainfall and its consumption by the agricultural communities. If we consider that one hamburger takes about 635 gallons of water to produce the problem becomes clear. To look at water consumption at a different level the average American household uses 107,000 gallons per day (2012). Rainfall not only replenishes ground water supplies but also provides for year-round water sources for many communities by replenishing snow to mountains in the winter that in turn provides water in the summer.

Depletion of Minerals

Materials from the Earth provide for human needs such as food, clothing, and housing. Some of the materials needed are renewable resources, such as agricultural and forestry products, while others are nonrenewable, such as minerals. The following table shows the life expectancy of critical minerals used by today's technologies and extractable at a reasonable cost. (Meadows, Donella et all)

Once these minerals are depleted, it will be extremely expensive to extract them and, therefore, a substantial rise in the cost of needed human commodities and services will be incurred that is beyond the reach of many.

In addition, the scarcer the mineral becomes, the deeper we tend to dig for it, disfiguring the earth and taking it out of the natural cycles of rejuvenation.

```
Mineral        Years Remaining

Silver         15
Lead           17
Zinc           20
Copper         22
Tin            28
Nickel         30
Iron           65
Aluminum       81
```

Life expectancy table of economically extractable minerals.

Global Warming (Archer, David)

If you prepare a large capped glass flask containing ordinary air, a green piece of filter paper inside of it and expose it to the rays of the Sun, the temperature inside of it will rise due to the different gasses in the air and the color of the filter paper.

If you add pure carbon dioxide to the above glass flask, the temperature inside of it will rise more quickly and become warmer. If you add pure methane, you will find that the warming effect is 21 times that of carbon dioxide. Similarly, if you add pure nitrous oxide, the warming effect is 330 times that of carbon dioxide.

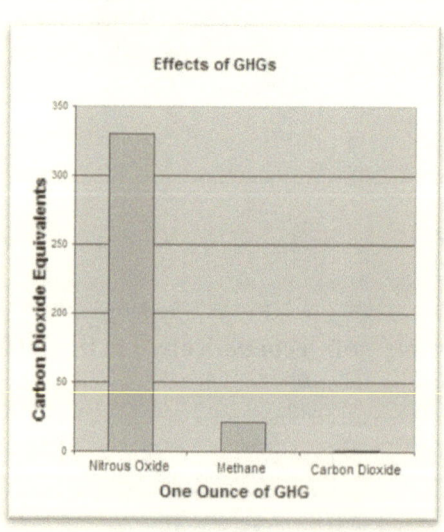

The effects of different greenhouse gasses on temperature in controlled conditions in the laboratory.

If you start with two capped glass flasks both containing ordinary air and green pieces of filter paper, add a little water to each of the green filter papers and to one add greenhouse gasses, the water will evaporate with greater speed in the flask with the greenhouse gasses, leaving the filter paper dryer.

Similarly, if you add ice to both flasks, the ice in the flask with the greenhouse gasses will melt much faster than the ice in the air only flask.

Today we are at the very early stages of global warming and its effects, but there are signs that we are on the road to major changes in weather and ocean patterns.

Indeed, the water vapor content of the air is rising as can be seen in the above graph showing an average increase in water vapor of .04 parts per million per year over Boulder, Colorado.

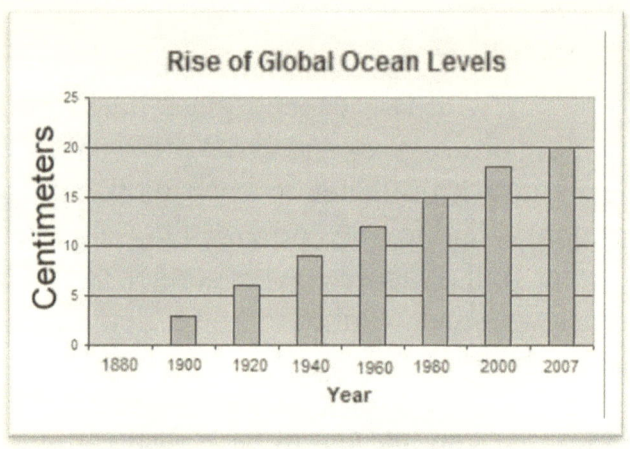

Actual sea level changes over the last 100 years.

Indeed, lower latitude glaciers are melting away to the point that only 50% of them remain on Earth since the year 1900. There are many agricultural communities dependent on the annual melting of glacier ice and its replenishment.

In addition, the ocean and sea levels have been rising at the rate of an inch every ten years and are now accelerating.

In the United States of America, forest fires are burning larger sections of land and are reaching higher up the mountains where there was once snow to slow them down. These fires are also burning hotter and trees such as the Ponderosa

Pines, trees that depend on fires, are dying from the extreme heat the fires generate.

In addition, nitrous oxides play important roles in atmospheric chemistry. They are emitted to the atmosphere naturally, mainly as a result of microbial activities in soils and lightning discharges. Currently and predominantly, the emissions occur as a result of human activities (such as the combustion of fossil fuels, biomass burning and the use of fertilizers). Long-term trends of its concentration in the atmosphere are not documented adequately. Nevertheless, reconstructed emission inventories suggest that large increases have occurred throughout this century. Exposures to nitrous oxides have direct adverse effects on humans, animals and plants. Nitrous oxides also contribute to the global environmental problems facing our planet (i.e., excessive global warming, depletion of the ozone layer and acid rain).

Antibiotics and the Superbugs (Schmidt, Michael A.)

Antibiotic resistance is a serious and growing problem in today's medical industry and has become one of the imminent public health concerns of this century. In the simplest cases, drug-resistant organisms acquire resistance by mutations that make them immune to common antibiotics, thereby requiring the use of less common secondary antibiotics. Primary antibiotics are preferred because they have several advantages that include safety, availability and cost. Secondary antibiotics are broader in spectrum, possess higher risk and may be more expensive or locally unavailable. In the case of some multiple drug resistant pathogens, resistance to secondary and even tertiary antibiotics have been demonstrated, illustrated by pathogens Staphylococcus aureus and Pseudomonas aeruginosa (which possess a high level of intrinsic resistance).

The major cause of wide-spread antibiotic resistance is the overuse of antibiotics in agriculture and in the human health field. It is becoming harder and harder to fight infections caused by these drug-resistant pathogens and their increase in number and prevalence is outpacing man's ability to fight them.

Chapter 7

Is There Going to be another "Mass Extinction" Event on Earth?

A mass extinction (or biotic crisis) is a widespread and rapid decrease in the amount of life on Earth. This loss of life is expressed as the percentage of species that die off within a short time frame. The level of species die-off in a mass extinction is estimated to be about 50% according to some researchers.

The majority of life's diversity and biomass on Earth is microbial, but microbes have no skeletons to leave behind and thus difficult to measure. Therefore, recorded extinction events are influenced by the easily observed, biologically complex organisms that leave behind skeletons.

In the past 540 million years it has been estimated that there have been five major extinctions when over 50% of animal species died. The following is a list of those extinctions:

1.   Cretaceous–Paleogene extinction event: 66 million years ago. About 75% of all species became extinct. In the seas it reduced the percentage of sessile animals to about 33%. All non-avian dinosaurs became extinct during that time.

2.   Triassic–Jurassic extinction event: 200 million years ago. About 70% to 75% of all species became extinct.

3.   Permian–Triassic extinction event: 251 million years ago. Earth's largest extinction killed 90% to 96% of all species

4.   Late Devonian extinction event: 375–360 million years ago. About 70% of all species became extinct. This extinction event lasted perhaps as long as 20 million years, and there is evidence for a series of extinction pulses within this period.

5.   Ordovician–Silurian extinction event: 450–440 million years ago. Two events occurred that killed off 60% to 70% of all species. Together they are ranked by many scientists as the second largest of the five major extinctions in Earth's history in terms of percentage of genera that went extinct.

Trying to determine what happened by reading the fossil evidence is very difficult. It is as if you had a huge old-fashioned movie reel of a film of the Earth for the last 500 million years that had been damaged by an acid spill that destroyed 90% of it. All you had left was a frame here and frame there with which to explain the plot.

There are also other problems reading the fissile record. The older the fossil record gets, the more difficult it is to read. This is because, older fossils are usually buried at a considerable depth in the rock and harder to get to, dating older fossils is more difficult, productive fossil beds are researched more often than unproductive ones that might have important clues, the deposition process can be disturbed by prehistoric environmental disturbances, the preservation of fossils varies on land, but marine fossils tend to be better preserved.

Summary

As you recall from the section on the long algae blooms in a pond, it is a common growth trend and humans are simply following the programs coded into their genetics and language information systems down a similar path. In the pond example, all life was extinguished except for the bacteria consuming the dead material left behind, and in the massive extinction examples, total loss of life on Earth was 50% or more. Will the effects of the human "bloom" be the same, more or less than that of the long algae bloom of a massive extinction?

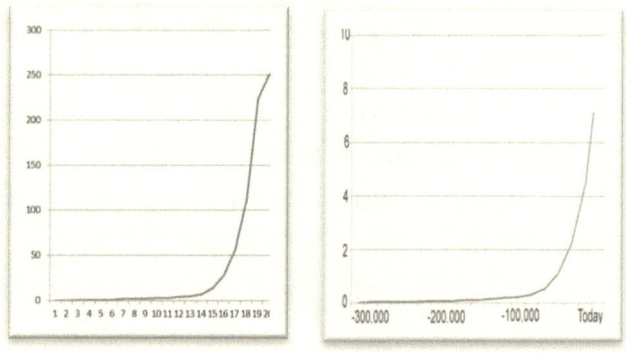

A comparison of population density over time (vertical side) between algae undergoing a bloom (left) and humankind undergoing exponential growth.

Chapter 8

Will Human Activities Cause or Deter the Next Mass Extinction?

A 2014 study in the journal Science (published by the American Association for the Advancement of Science) found that species of plants and animals are becoming extinct at least 1,000 times faster than they did before humans appeared 200,000 years ago. Human impacts on the quantity and variation in animal species are not well understood by the general public. Among vertebrates that walk on land, 322 species have become extinct since 1500 A.D. and populations of the remaining species show a 25% decline in abundance (Doyle Rice, USA TODAY 6:32 p.m. EDT July 24, 2014).

What's new about this extinction is that the driving force is not a meteorite or a mega-volcanic eruption but one species: Homo sapiens.

The decline of fauna and flora around the world is caused by habitat loss (due to human population growth, expansion, and competition), invasions by other non-native species and global climate disruptions (due to greenhouse gasses).

On the other hand, there are scientific and non-scientific predictions that the human population will experience a drastic decline in the coming twenty to fifty years. One such study is detailed in the book entitled *Limits to Growth* (Meadows, Donella et al) in which the population of humans will drop by 50% or more in the next thirty years or so, along with a ten-fold decline in the human welfare index compared to today.

Whether this or another predictor of human decline comes about, will it be enough to save the planet Earth from the next mass extinction?

Chapter 9

Conclusion

Life is the process of a chemical compound toppling over other structures in order to build up its own. This toppling and building process requires energy and on Earth this energy comes mostly from the Sun.

This progression must follow the physics laws of entropy which state, "Entropy is a thermodynamic quantity representing the unavailability of a system's thermal energy for conversion into mechanical work, often interpreted as the degree of disorder or randomness in the system" so says the Oxford dictionary.

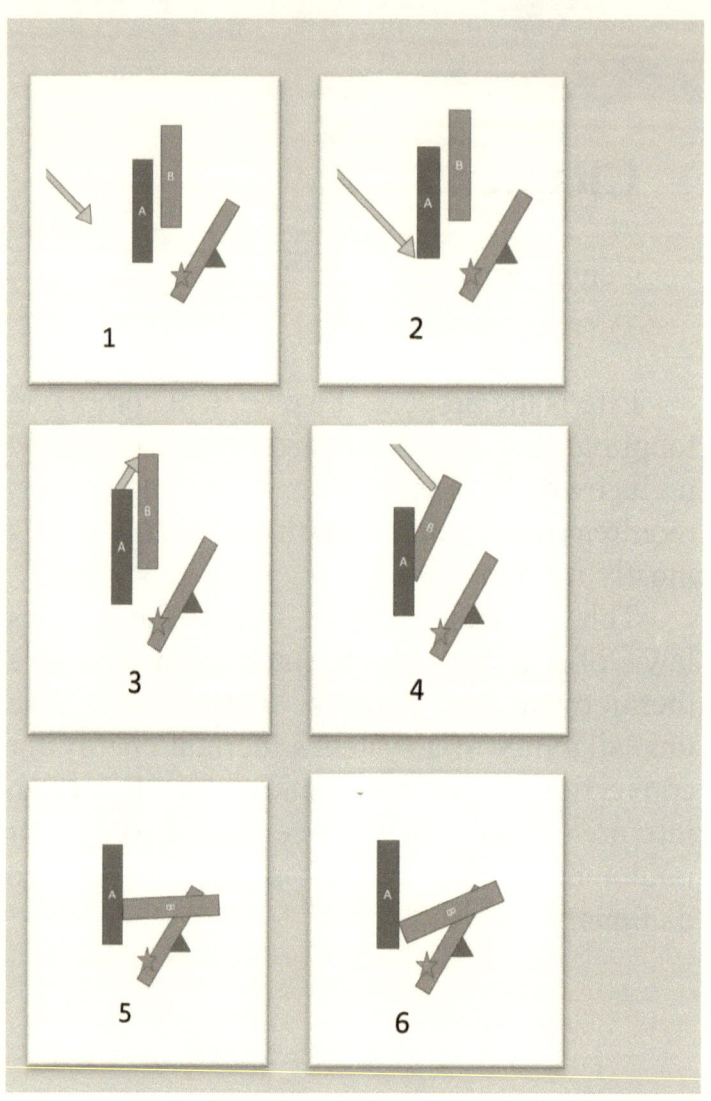

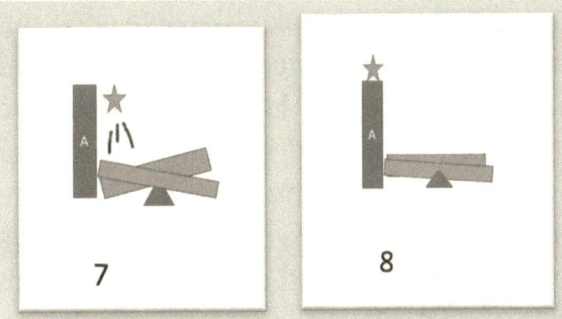

Example: A Star is Born

Imagine two pillars of reflective plastic foam A and B standing side by side. In front of them is a teetertotter (or a seesaw if you will) with a star on the low side and the low side is in front of Pillar A. At this point the two pillars, the star and teetertotter are a system at an entropy value of 1. And let's also say there is a beam of light from the Sun hurtling towards the base of pillar A. Include that beam of light as part of the system.

Now imagine the beam of light bouncing off of base of pillar A and hitting the top of pillar B toppling it over onto the high end of the teetertotter which then tosses up the star which lands on top of pillar A causing it to become alive. In addition, the teetertotter falls to the ground. The star on top of pillar A reduces entropy to 0 because it is an increase in order. The toppling of pillar B increases disorder to an entropy value of 1 again and the falling of the teetertotter increases disorder to the entropy value of 2.

Nature does not speak like we do but communicates by chemical reactions that follow the laws of physics. Humans do not have to carry the burden of guilt as many do for the upcoming biotic catastrophe. After all we are also reacting chemicals obeying the natural laws of physics. So, sit back and enjoy the ride with music, song and dance for we are on a rudderless ship and mother nature holds the secret to where we are going.

The End

www.ingramcontent.com/pod-product-compliance
Lightning Source LLC
Chambersburg PA
CBHW050344290526
45785CB00006B/2626